LET'S CELEBRATE

Abraham Lincoln

and Presidents' Day

by Joanne Barkan
pictures by Lyle Miller

Silver Press

In memory of Michael Harrington

Produced by Kirchoff/Wohlberg, Inc.
Text copyright © 1990 Kirchoff/Wohlberg, Inc.
Illustrations copyright © 1990 Lyle Miller and
Kirchoff/Wohlberg, Inc.

Published by Silver Press, a division of Silver Burdett Press, Inc.
Simon & Schuster, Inc., Prentice Hall Bldg., Englewood Cliffs, NJ 07632

Printed in the United States of America

10 9 8 7 6 5 4 3 2 1

Library of Congress Cataloging-in-Publication Data
Barkan, Joanne.
Abraham Lincoln and Presidents' Day / by Joanne Barkan: pictures
by Lyle Miller.
p. cm.—(Let's celebrate)
Summary: Discusses the accomplishments of Abraham Lincoln and why
he deserves to be recognized on Presidents' Day.
1. Lincoln, Abraham, 1809-1865—Juvenile literature.
2. Presidents—United States—Biography—Juvenile literature.
3. Presidents' Day—Juvenile literature. [1. Lincoln, Abraham,
1809-1865. 2. Presidents. 3. Presidents' Day.] I. Miller, Lyle.
1950-   ill. II. Title. III. Series.
E457.905.B26 1990
973.7'092—dc20   89-49542
[B]   CIP
[92]   AC
ISBN 0-671-69113-9   ISBN 0-671-69107-4 (lib. bdg.)

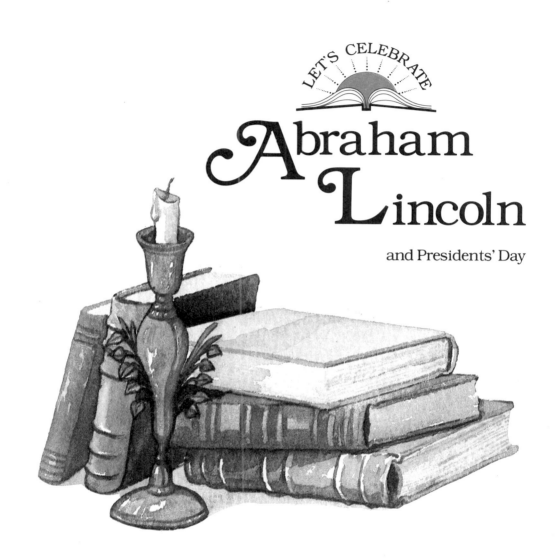

LET'S CELEBRATE

Abraham
Lincoln

and Presidents' Day

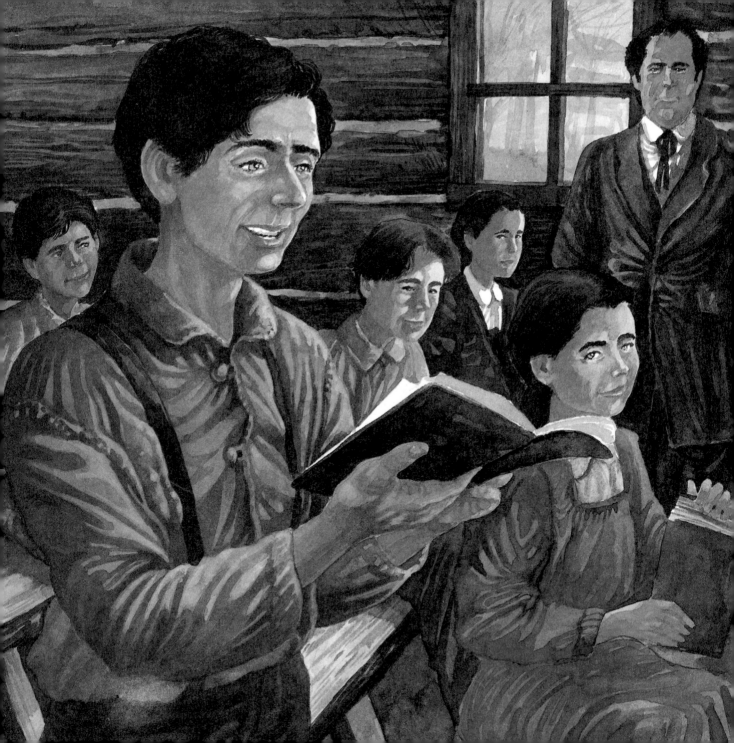

Growing Up

"What's that you're writing, Abe Lincoln?"

Abe's sister Sarah leaned over. She looked in Abe's homemade notebook.

"*Sh-sh!*" Abe whispered. But it was too late.

"Abraham Lincoln!" The schoolmaster's voice boomed. "Stand and read what you've written."

Abe's voice shook as he read:

Abraham Lincoln
his hand and pen
he will be good but
God knows when.

Everyone in the room laughed, except the schoolmaster. He stared at Abraham. This boy was the best student he had ever met. Abe read well. He was good at arithmetic. He loved to learn.

"So now you're writing poems," the schoolmaster said. Then he added, "You won't be coming to school much longer this year, will you?"

Abe shook his head. "This is my last day," he said. "The fields are ready for plowing."

Abraham Lincoln went to school just a few weeks each year. The rest of the time, his father needed him to work on the farm.

"I won't miss walking these four miles twice a day," Sarah said.

Abe pulled his jacket tighter against the wind. "I don't mind it," he said.

"I know!" Sarah laughed. "You don't mind walking eight miles to borrow a book either!"

When they reached home, Abe quickly pulled a book out of his pocket.

"Sorry, Son," his father said. "There's no time for reading now. You have chores to do."

"Well," Abe said, "I'll chop wood for the fire. I'll get water from the well. I'll take care of the cow and horse. Then if I have any time left, I'll read my book." Abe looked at Sarah and winked. They both knew there wouldn't be any time left.

Later that evening, Abe was lying in bed. His stepmother, Sally, came to see him. "What book did you want to read this afternoon?" she asked.

"*The Life of Washington*," Abe answered. "It's about the first president of the United States. He's the greatest man I've ever read about."

"You keep reading whenever you can, Abe," his stepmother said. "It's a good thing."

"I will," Abe said. "I don't want to be a farmer. And I don't want to live here in the woods. I want to see if I can do more."

"Work hard," Sally answered, "and you will."

Traveling

Six years went by. One day, Abe's friends were walking in the woods. Their names were John and Nat.

"Listen to that noise!" John said.

WHACK! C-r-e-e-a-k. CRASH!

"Sounds like men chopping down trees," Nat said.

"Nope," John replied. "It's just Abe Lincoln."

John was right. They found Abe swinging his axe against a large tree. Abe was now nineteen years old. He was taller and stronger than any man for miles around.

"Abe!" Nat called. "We've come to hear about your trip to Rockport. Tell us what happened."

"I visited the courthouse," Abe said.

Then he jumped onto the stump of a tree. He began waving his arms and making a speech. He sounded just like the lawyers in court.

"Does that boy look like a pig thief?" Abe shouted. He pointed at John. "Yes, he does!"

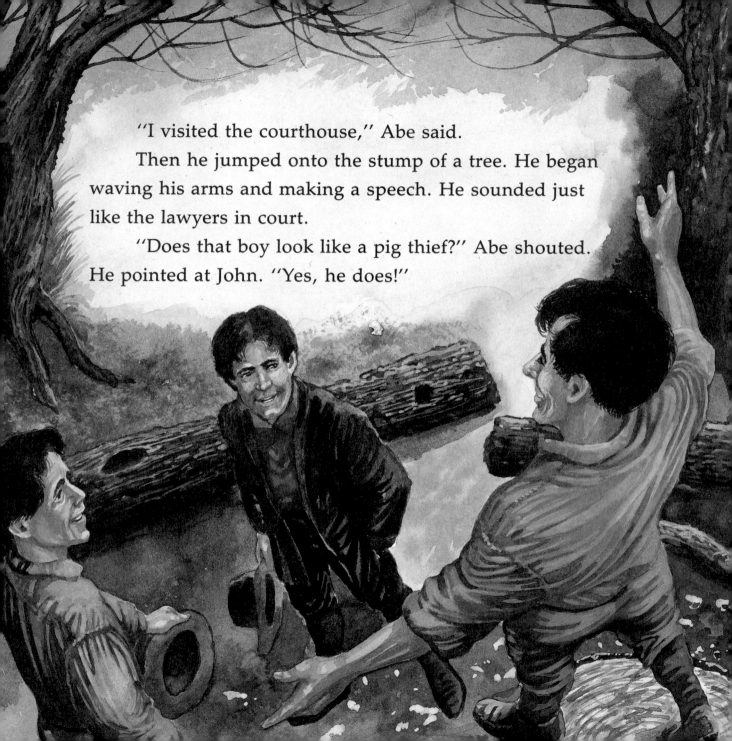

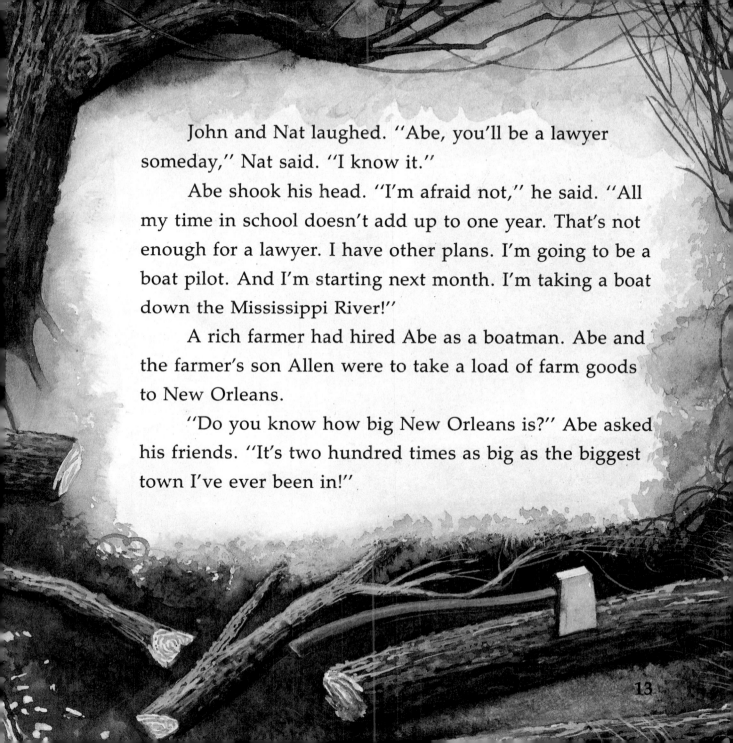

John and Nat laughed. "Abe, you'll be a lawyer someday," Nat said. "I know it."

Abe shook his head. "I'm afraid not," he said. "All my time in school doesn't add up to one year. That's not enough for a lawyer. I have other plans. I'm going to be a boat pilot. And I'm starting next month. I'm taking a boat down the Mississippi River!"

A rich farmer had hired Abe as a boatman. Abe and the farmer's son Allen were to take a load of farm goods to New Orleans.

"Do you know how big New Orleans is?" Abe asked his friends. "It's two hundred times as big as the biggest town I've ever been in!"

In April, it was time to start the trip. Abe stood on the riverbank. Allen was on the flatboat.

"Let's get moving!" Allen shouted to him.

For the next two months, the flatboat was their home on the river.

Then one morning, Abe called out, "There it is! New Orleans! We've come twelve hundred miles! Let's push into shore right away."

"Look at all the flatboats," Allen said. "There must be a thousand of them!"

"And sailing ships, too!" Abe said.

Allen and Abe sold their goods quickly. They wanted to see more of New Orleans. As they walked, they saw things they had never seen before.

"Houses are made of brick, not logs. And they're four stories tall!" said Allen.

15

Abe was quiet. He was looking at something else. It was something he would never forget.

"That man is selling Negroes [black people]!" he finally said. "This is a slave market."

A white man stood on a platform. He was pointing to a girl sitting at his feet. She was black. She had heavy chains around her ankles.

"Don't sell my girl!" a woman on the platform cried. "Don't take my child away from me!"

Abe was angry. "People can't be sold like cattle," he thought. "This must be stopped."

A Famous Lawyer

Many years passed. A crowd stood outside a small courthouse in Illinois. The door to the courthouse opened.

"There he is!" a boy shouted. He pointed to a very tall man. "It's Abraham Lincoln!"

Mr. Lincoln walked over to the boy. He shook his hand. "Nice to meet you," he said. "I have a son who is just your age."

The boy was quiet for a moment. Then he burst out, "My mother says you're the best lawyer in the state!"

Lincoln smiled as he got into his buggy. He waved good-bye to the boy. Then he rode off toward home.

Lincoln spotted three faces in the front window as he rode up to his large wooden house. The next thing he knew, the door flew open. His children ran down the porch steps to meet him.

After dinner, Lincoln played marbles with Willie. He told his wife Mary and son Robert about his court cases.

"It's time for bed," Mary said to her sons. "Go up now!"

Lincoln picked up his newspaper. As he read, his face grew sad.

"What's wrong?" Mary asked.

"There is a new law that will allow more slavery in the United States.

"I once saw a little slave girl taken from her mother and sold. I have never forgotten her."

Lincoln took Mary's hands. "I must work against the new slavery law."

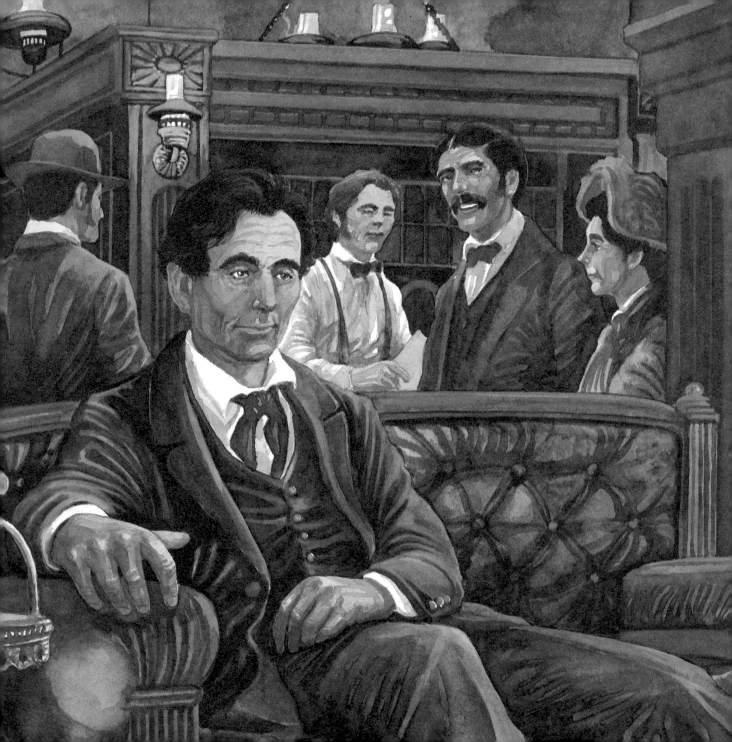

A Great President

Six years went by. Abraham Lincoln worked hard to stop slavery from spreading. He gave speeches all over Illinois. He became famous in the rest of the country, too. The people who wanted to stop slavery liked Lincoln. They thought he should be president. Lincoln agreed to run in the next election.

One evening in 1860, Lincoln walked into the town's telegraph office. He sat down on an old sofa. He stretched out his long legs.

"Aren't you nervous?" asked his friend. "You're waiting to find out if you've been elected president of the United States!"

Just then the telegraph began clicking a message. Lincoln's friend read it. Then he began to shout at the top of his lungs. "You've won! You've won! You will be our next president!"

A large crowd was waiting outside. When they heard the news, the men threw their hats into the air. They set off fireworks. "Three cheers for President Lincoln!" they shouted.

Soon after Lincoln became president, a war between the states began. Lincoln's job was to end the war. He wanted to keep the states together as one country. He also had to help free the slaves.

The war had gone on for two years. On New Year's Day, 1863, Lincoln and his wife gave a holiday party at the White House.

The president greeted each guest. "Hello," he said again and again. He shook so many hands that his arm began to hurt.

After a while, Lincoln walked up to a few people. "It's time," he said. They left the room quietly. They went to Lincoln's office.

26

Everyone sat around a big oak table. In front of the president was a large piece of paper.

In a clear voice, Lincoln read what was written on the paper. "I order and declare that all slaves are forever free!"

Then the president picked up a gold pen. His arm was so tired that the pen shook. He dipped it in ink. Then he wrote his name on the paper.

"The slaves are now free!" one man cheered.

MAP OF
RGINIA

28

Another looked at what the president had written. "You always sign your name A. Lincoln," he said. "Why did you write Abraham Lincoln today?"

"Because today, I have done the best thing I will ever do in my life," the president said.

29

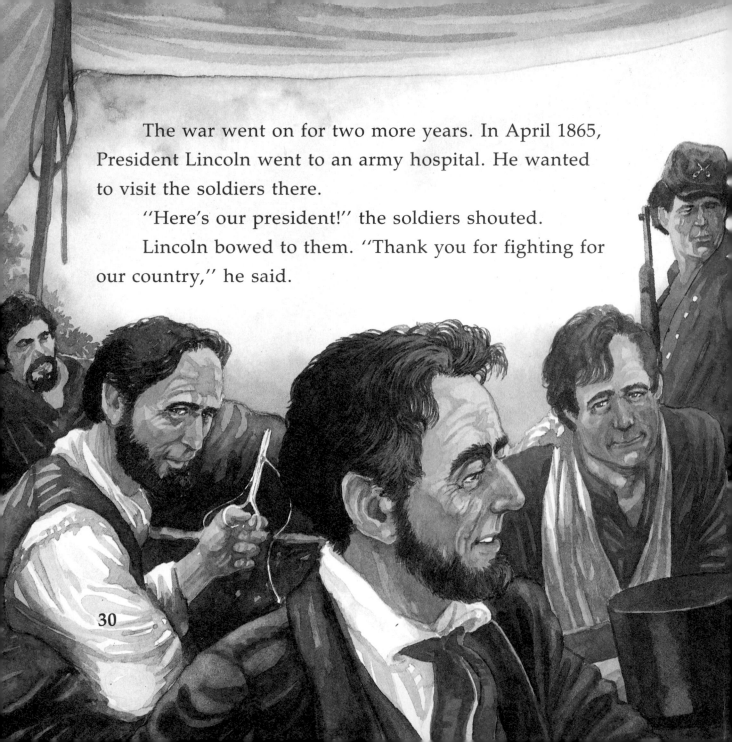

The war went on for two more years. In April 1865, President Lincoln went to an army hospital. He wanted to visit the soldiers there.

"Here's our president!" the soldiers shouted.

Lincoln bowed to them. "Thank you for fighting for our country," he said.

Lincoln shook hands with every soldier.

"What's your name?" he would ask. "Where do you come from?"

"We've heard the war is almost over," said one soldier. "Our side has won."

"Yes," Lincoln said. "The other side has given up."

"Will we punish them for making war?" another soldier asked.

"No," Lincoln said. "We must not be angry. We must be kind. Our country has been hurt, just as you have been. We must heal in peace."

31

Abraham Lincoln was a wise and gentle man.
He was one of our country's greatest leaders.
He lived to see the end of the war. But sadly, a short
time later he was shot and killed while watching a
play at Ford's Theater in Washington, D.C.